Clementine A. Fortier

The Interesting weird fact For curious smart minds

Contents

1. Introduction 1

2. Pop culture 3

3. Technology 10

4. Animals...13

5. Inventions 16

6. Movie..19

7. Planets..23

8. Country 26

9. History 29

10. Science..33

11. Strange creatures 36

1.

2.

3.

4.

5.

6.

7.

8.

9.

10.

1

Introduction

In the vast expanse of human knowledge, there exists a realm where the peculiar and the extraordinary converge, captivating the minds of the curious and the intellects of the smart. Welcome to the enthralling universe of "Very Interesting Weird Facts for Curious Smart Minds." Embark on a journey through the corridors of knowledge where the conventional gives way to the extraordinary, and the mundane transforms into the extraordinary.

In this collection, we delve into the peculiar tapestry of facts that defy the ordinary, each tidbit carefully curated to pique the interest of the inquisitive mind. It is a symphony of eccentricity, a celebration of the oddities that make the world a kaleidoscope of fascinating wonders. From the enigmatic depths of the ocean to the boundless expanse of outer space, these facts beckon the reader to explore the unknown and challenge preconceived notions.

As we navigate this intellectual odyssey, be prepared to unravel the mysteries behind the seemingly mundane aspects of life. What if I told you that the humble honeybee performs a dance that communicates intricate details about the location of nectar? Or that there exists a species of jellyfish capable of reverting its aging process, a biological enigma that defies the very essence of mortality?

Our exploration doesn't stop with the natural world; we extend our gaze to the realms of history, where the peculiarities of the past come to life. Discover the riveting tale of Rasputin, the mystic advisor to the Russian royal family, whose resilience to poison became the stuff of legends. Uncover the secrets of the ancient city of Pompeii, frozen in time by the catastrophic eruption of Mount Vesuvius, preserving the daily lives of its inhabitants for millennia.

Prepare to have your perception of reality challenged as we explore the frontiers of science and technology. From mind-bending quantum phenomena to cutting-edge innovations, these weird facts will leave you marveling at the boundless potential of human ingenuity. Did you know that scientists have successfully teleport ed information from one location to another through the mysterious world of quantum entanglement? It's a revelation that blurs the line between science fiction and scientific fact.

In the spirit of intellectual curiosity, "Very Interesting Weird Facts for Curious Smart Minds" transcends the ordinary, inviting readers to embrace the unconventional and question the status quo. As we navigate this captivating odyssey, we encourage you to approach each fact with an open mind, for it is through the lens of curiosity that we unlock the door to a world where the weird and wonderful reign supreme.

Join us on this extraordinary expedition through the annals of knowledge, where the pursuit of wisdom is intertwined with the joy of discovering the delightfully strange. Buckle up, dear reader, as we embark on a thrilling adventure that transcends the boundaries of the known and ventures into the uncharted territories of the remarkably weird.

2

Pop culture

The term "pop culture" is short for popular culture, encompassing trends, ideas, images, and phenomena that are prevalent in mainstream society.

The Beatles hold the record for the most No. 1 hits on the Billboard Hot 100 chart, with 20 chart-toppers.

The iconic "Star Wars" franchise was initially inspired by old samurai films and Flash Gordon serials.

Michael Jackson's "Thriller" album is the best-selling album of all time, with over 66 million copies sold worldwide.

The first-ever comic book superhero is widely considered to be Superman, created by Jerry Siegel and Joe Shuster in 1938.

The term "meme" was coined by British evolutionary biologist Richard Dawkins in his 1976 book "The Selfish Gene."

The concept of the "selfie" was popularized by Australian photographer David Slater in 2011.

The word "dude" originated in the 19th century as a term for a well-dressed man, and it evolved to its modern usage in the 20th century.

The world's first feature-length animated film is "Snow White and the Seven Dwarfs," released by Disney in 1937.

The term "fandom" refers to a subculture of fans who are intensely devoted to a particular area of pop culture, such as a TV show, movie, or book series.

The concept of virtual reality (VR) was popularized in the '80s and '90s but has recently seen a resurgence with advancements in technology.

The first video game character to become a cultural icon is Mario, created by Nintendo and first appearing in the game "Donkey Kong" in 1981.

The term "mashup" originally referred to a musical genre that combines elements from different songs. Now, it's used more broadly to describe any combination of disparate elements.

The fictional language Klingon, spoken by the Klingon species in "Star Trek," has a fully developed grammar and vocabulary.

The "Dab" dance move gained popularity in the hip-hop and sports communities and was first introduced by rapper Skippa Da Flippa.

The term "cosplay" is a portmanteau of the words "costume" and "play," and it refers to the practice of dressing up as a character from a movie, book, or video game.

The word "manga" comes from the Japanese words for "whimsical drawings" and refers to Japanese comic books and graphic novels.

The term "emo" originally referred to a style of emotionally expressive punk rock music but later evolved to describe a fashion and lifestyle subculture.

The world's first recorded graffiti artist is considered to be Kilroy, a fictional character created by American soldiers during World War II.

The first-ever emoji was created by Japanese artist Shigetaka Kurita in 1999.

The term "cyberpunk" describes a subgenre of science fiction that combines high-tech, futuristic elements with a gritty, dystopian atmosphere.

The Guinness World Record for the largest gathering of people dressed as Harry Potter characters is 997, set in 2015.

The dance move "The Floss" gained popularity through the video game "Fortnite" and was popularized by the backpack-wearing character known as "Backpack Kid."

The term "geek" originally referred to a carnival performer who bit the heads off chickens but has evolved to describe someone deeply passionate about a specific interest, often related to pop culture.

The "Dungeons & Dragons" role-playing game, first published in 1974, played a significant role in shaping modern fantasy literature and gaming.

The term "Otaku" in Japan refers to a person with obsessive interests, particularly in anime and manga.

The phrase "May the Force be with you" from "Star Wars" has become a cultural catchphrase, expressing good luck or encouragement.

The first-ever music video aired on MTV was "Video Killed the Radio Star" by The Buggles in 1981.

The term "steampunk" refers to a genre of speculative fiction that incorporates steam-powered machinery and aesthetics inspired by 19th-century industrial steam-powered machinery.

The term "frenemy" refers to a person who pretends to be a friend but is actually a rival or competitor.

The term "cyberspace" was coined by science fiction writer William Gibson in his novel "Neuromancer."

The concept of "viral marketing" involves creating content that spreads rapidly and widely online, often through social media.

The "Keep Calm and Carry On" poster, now a popular meme, was originally created by the British government in 1939 as a motivational message during World War II.

The first-ever product to have a barcode was a pack of Wrigley's chewing gum.

The term "fomo" stands for "fear of missing out" and refers to the anxiety that one might miss out on an exciting event or experience.

The concept of a "mashup" in music gained popularity with DJ Danger Mouse's album "The Grey Album," which combined tracks from The Beatles and Jay-Z.

The word "hipster" originally referred to people in the 1940s who were associated with jazz and rejected mainstream culture.

The term "fan fiction" refers to stories written by fans that use characters or settings from existing works of fiction.

The "Rickroll" meme involves tricking someone into clicking a hyperlink that leads to the music video for Rick Astley's "Never Gonna Give You Up."

The term "vlog" is short for "video blog," and it refers to a blog that primarily uses video content.

The term "podcast" is a combination of "iPod" and "broadcast," reflecting the medium's association with portable media players.

The term "troll" originally referred to a mythical creature but has evolved to describe a person who deliberately provokes and upsets others online.

The term "GIF" stands for "Graphics Interchange Format" and refers to a type of image file that supports animated images.

The first documented flash mob occurred in 2003 when a group in New York City coordinated to freeze in place at a specific time in Grand Central Station.

The term "LARP" stands for "live-action role-playing," where participants physically act out their characters' actions.

The first-ever computer virus was created in 1983 and was called the "Elk Cloner." It spread to Apple II computers through infected floppy disks.

The term "remix" originally referred to reimagining and reworking music but has expanded to include various forms of media.

The term "twerking" gained widespread attention after Miley Cyrus's performance at the 2013 MTV Video Music Awards.

The term "Goth" refers to a subculture that emerged in the late 1970s, characterized by its dark and mysterious aesthetic.

The term "mumble rap" describes a style of hip-hop characterized by its relaxed delivery and often unclear enunciation.

The term "Lolcat" refers to humorous images of cats with captions written in deliberately broken English.

The first-ever commercially successful video game was "Pong," released by Atari in 1972.

The term "reboot" refers to restarting or refreshing a franchise by creating new versions of existing stories or characters.

The concept of the "man cave" refers to a dedicated space, often in a home, where a man can pursue his hobbies and interests.

The term "webisode" refers to a short episode of a web-based series, typically released online.

The term "emojis" were first introduced in Japan in the late 1990s and have since become a ubiquitous form of digital communication.

The term "fandom shipping" involves fans expressing a desire for two characters to enter into a romantic relationship.

The first-ever computer mouse was invented by Douglas Engelbart in 1964 and was made of wood.

The term "augmented reality" (AR) refers to technology that overlays digital information on the real-world environment.

The term "internet meme" refers to a piece of content, such as an image or video, that spreads rapidly online and often evolves as it is shared.

The term "cyberbullying" refers to the use of electronic communication to harass or intimidate others.

The first-ever 3D feature film was "Avatar," directed by James Cameron and released in 2009.

The term "emo rap" combines elements of emotional and confessional lyrics with rap music.

The concept of "binge-watching" became popular with the rise of streaming services, allowing viewers to watch multiple episodes of a TV series in one sitting.

The term "clickbait" refers to online content designed to attract attention and encourage users to click on a link.

The term "planking" involves lying face down in an unusual or unexpected location and posting a photo of it online.

The term "catfish" refers to a person who creates a fake online identity to deceive others.

The term "geocaching" combines outdoor adventure with GPS technology, as participants use GPS coordinates to find hidden containers, or "caches."

The term "spoiler alert" warns readers or viewers that information about the plot or ending of a story will be revealed.

The term "vape" refers to inhaling and exhaling vapor produced by an electronic cigarette or   similar   device.

3

Technology

The first computer mouse was made of wood.

The world's first computer programmer was Ada Lovelace in the 1800s.

The term "bug" in computer science originated when an actual moth caused a malfunction in an early computer.

The Apollo 11 guidance computer that landed humans on the moon had less processing power than a modern-day smartphone.

The first webcam was created to monitor a coffee pot at the University of Cambridge.

The world's first electronic digital computer was the ENIAC, which weighed about 27 tons.

The term "WI-Fi" doesn't actually stand for anything; it's just a brand name.

The first text message ever sent was "Merry Christmas" in 1992.

The average smartphone has more computing power than the computers used for the Apollo 11 moon landing.

The first computer virus was created in 1983 and was called the Elk Cloner.

The concept of the World Wide Web was proposed by Tim Berners-Lee in 1989.

The first 1GB hard drive was announced by IBM in 1980 and weighed about 550 pounds.

The computer mouse was invented by Douglas Engelbart in 1964.

The word "robot" comes from the Czech word "robota," meaning forced labor.

The first computer game, Spacewar!, was created in 1962.

The first electronic computer, the Atanasoff-Berry Computer (ABC), was completed in 1942.

The world's first computer virus for PCs was created in 1986 and was called Brain.

The term "hack" originated at MIT and referred to a prank or clever programming trick.

The first website ever created is still online. It was launched by Tim Berners-Lee in 1991.

The concept of email existed before the World Wide Web, with the first system developed in the 1960s.

The first computer-generated music was created in 1951 by the CSIRAC computer in Australia.

The first computer animation was made in 1962 and involved a bouncing ball.

The first computer to defeat a reigning world chess champion was IBM's Deep Blue in 1997.

The world's first computer, the Antikythera mechanism, dates back to ancient Greece (150-100 BCE).

The term "cloud computing" was coined by Compaq in 1996.

The first domain name ever registered was symbolics.com on March 15, 1985.

The first computer virus that spread in the wild was the Morris Worm in 1988.

The first computer password was "login."

The first computer with a graphical user interface (GUI) was the Xerox Alto in 1973.

The first 1TB hard drive was introduced by Seagate in 2007.

The world's first computer animation was created by John Whitney in 1960.

The QWERTY keyboard layout was designed in 1873 for typewriters to prevent jamming.

The term "firewall" originally referred to a wall designed to confine a fire.

The first computer to use integrated circuits was the IBM 360 in 1964.

The first computer mouse had two wheels and was called the "X-Y Position Indicator for a Display System."

The first computer virus to infect PCs was the Creeper virus in 1971.

The term "Bluetooth" comes from a 10th-century Danish king, Harald "Bluetooth" Gormsson.

The first computer with a hard drive was the IBM 305 RAMAC in 1956.

The first computer virus for Windows was WinVir in 1992.

The first computer-generated feature film was "Toy Story" by Pixar in 1995.

The first computer mouse with a ball instead of wheels was introduced in 1972.

The world's first computer art exhibition took place in 1965.

The first computer to use a mouse and graphical user interface was the Apple Lisa in 1983.

The first computer to play music was the CSIRAC in 1951.

The first computer chess program was written in 1956 by Alex Bernstein.

The first computer designed for personal use was the Altair 8800 in 1975.

The first computer bug was a moth found in the Harvard Mark II computer in 1947.

The first computer to be controlled by software was the UNIVAC I in 1951.

The first computer game with graphics was "Spacewar!" in 1962.

The first computer with a color display was the IBM 8566 in 1984.

The first computer mouse sold commercially was the Microsoft Mouse in 1983.

The first computer to be used in an election was the UNIVAC I in 1952.

The first computer-generated special effects in a movie were in "Westworld" in 1973.

The first computer to run Unix was the PDP-7 in 1969.

The first computer with a gigahertz processor was the AMD Athlon in 2000.

The first computer-generated TV series was "ReBoot" in 1994.

The first computer printer was invented by Charles Babbage in the 1800s.

The first computer to beat a world chess champion in a match was IBM's Deep Thought in 1989.

The first computer to use magnetic core memory was the UNIVAC I in 1951.

The first computer to use a graphical user interface and a mouse was the Xerox Star in 1981.

The first computer worm, the Morris Worm, caused significant internet disruption in 1988.

The first computer to run a video game was the Ferranti Mark I in 1952.

The first computer to have a built-in hard drive was the IBM 305 RAMAC in 1956.

The first computer to use a solid-state drive (SSD) was the IBM 3650 in 1973.

The first computer to use a graphical user interface, mouse, and ethernet was the Xerox Alto in 1973.

The first computer to be commercially available was the UNIVAC I in 1951.

The first computer to use a microprocessor was the Intel 4004 in 1971.

The first computer to have a touchscreen interface was the PLATO IV in 1972.

The first computer to be connected to the ARPANET (precursor to the internet) was the SDS Sigma 7 in 1969.

The first computer to run the Linux operating system was the DEC Alpha in 1993.

4

Animals

The mimic octopus can imitate the appearance and behaviors of more than 15 different marine species.

Elephants are capable of recognizing themselves in a mirror, showing a level of self-awareness.

The tongue of a blue whale can weigh as much as an elephant.

Cows have best friends and can become stressed when they are separated.

A single cow can produce about 200,000 glasses of milk in its lifetime.

Honey never spoils. Archaeologists have found pots of honey in ancient Egyptian tombs that are over 3,000 years old and still perfectly edible.

A group of flamingos is called a "flamboyance."

There are more species of beetles than there are plant species.

The archerfish can spit water up to 5 feet away to shoot down insects above the water's surface.

The mantis shrimp has the most complex eyes in the animal kingdom, with 16 types of color receptors.

A newborn kangaroo is the size of a lima bean and is not fully developed.

The cheetah is the fastest land animal, capable of reaching speeds up to 75 mph.

A snail can sleep for three years straight.

The only mammal capable of flight is the bat.

The tongue of a chameleon is twice the length of its body.

Pigs are highly intelligent animals, often outperforming dogs in certain cognitive tasks.

The fingerprints of a koala are so indistinguishable from humans that they have on occasion been confused at crime scenes in Australia.

A group of owls is called a "parliament."

A newborn kangaroo climbs into its mother's pouch, where it can continue developing.

The narwhal's tusk is an elongated tooth that can grow up to 10 feet long.

The axolotl, a type of salamander, has the remarkable ability to regrow entire limbs.

The mimicry skills of the stick insect make it almost invisible in its natural habitat.

Sea otters hold hands while sleeping to keep from drifting apart.

The golden poison dart frog's skin contains enough toxins to kill 10 grown men.

A group of jellyfish is called a "smack."

The pistol shrimp creates a bubble that reaches temperatures hotter than the surface of the sun when it snaps its claw shut.

The blue whale's heart is so large that a human could swim through its arteries.

Tardigrades, also known as water bears, are microscopic animals that can survive extreme conditions, including the vacuum of space.

The lyrebird can imitate the calls of other birds and even mimic chainsaws and camera shutters.

The hydra, a small freshwater organism, is biologically immortal and can regenerate indefinitely.

The male seahorse carries and gives birth to the offspring.

The geoduck, a type of clam, has one of the longest lifespans of any animal, living up to 146 years.

The brain of a goldfish has a memory span of about three seconds.

The axolotl can also regrow parts of its brain and heart.

A single gram of bat poop can contain up to 1.5 million microscopic fungi.

The male seahorse can give birth to up to 2,000 babies at once.

The mimic octopus can also imitate the appearance and behaviors of lionfish and flatfish.

Some frogs can survive being frozen and thawed, thanks to a natural antifreeze substance in their bodies.

The tongue of a blue whale can weigh as much as an elephant.

The African elephant is the largest land animal, and the Asian elephant is the second-largest.

The male seahorse is equipped with a specialized pouch to carry and nurture the developing eggs.

Cephalopods, such as octopuses and squids, have three hearts.

A group of crows is called a "murder."

The quokka, often referred to as the world's happiest animal, has a naturally smiling face.

Some species of ants use their own bodies to create living bridges for the colony to cross obstacles.

The tongue of a giraffe can be up to 45 centimeters long and is prehensile.

A newborn kangaroo is called a "joey."

The hummingbird is the only bird that can fly backward.

The regal horned lizard can shoot blood from its eyes as a defense mechanism.

A group of ravens is called an "unkindness."

The electric eel can produce electric shocks of up to 600 volts.

The echidna and the platypus are the only mammals that lay eggs.

The tongue of a blue whale is so large that 50 people could stand on it.

The bat is the only mammal capable of sustained flight.

The kangaroo is the only large animal that hops.

The axolotl is known for its ability to regenerate body parts, including its heart and spinal cord.

A group of ferrets is called a "business."

The blue-ringed octopus is one of the most venomous animals in the world.

The elephant's trunk has over 40,000 muscles.

The star-nosed mole has a nose with 22 appendages that can touch up to 12 objects per second.

The mimic octopus can change both its color and shape to imitate other marine animals.

The peregrine falcon is the fastest bird and can reach speeds of over 240 mph during a dive.

The thorny devil lizard can collect water on its skin by channeling it to its mouth.

The aye-aye, a type of lemur, uses its long middle finger to extract insects from tree bark.

A group of ferrets is known as a "business."

The hummingbird has the highest metabolism of any bird, requiring it to consume its own body weight in food every day.

The bombardier beetle can release a boiling chemical spray as a defense mechanism.

The praying mantis is the only insect that can turn its head 180 degrees.

The axolotl is a type of salamander that remains in its aquatic larval form throughout its life.

The Glaucus atlanticus, also known as the blue dragon, is a sea slug that can float on the surface of the water.

5

Inventions

The wheel, one of the most crucial inventions in history, dates back to around 3500 BC.

The invention of the printing press by Johannes Gutenberg in 1440 revolutionized the spread of information.

The concept of the steam engine, a key invention in the Industrial Revolution, was developed by Thomas Newcomen in 1712.

The first practical telephone was patented by Alexander Graham Bell in 1876.

The light bulb, attributed to Thomas Edison, was actually invented by a team of inventors, including Joseph Swan.

The microwave oven was invented accidentally when a researcher noticed a candy bar melting in his pocket due to microwaves.

The first computer mouse was invented by Douglas Engelbart in 1964.

The World Wide Web was invented by Sir Tim Berners-Lee in 1989.

The first camera was invented by Joseph Nicéphore Niépce in 1826, capturing the view from a window.

Velcro was invented by Swiss engineer George de Mestral, inspired by burrs sticking to his dog's fur.

The Frisbee was invented by Walter Morrison, who initially called it the "Pluto Platter."

The concept of the helicopter was envisioned by Leonardo da Vinci in the 15th century.

Ballpoint pens were invented by László Bíró, a Hungarian-Argentinian journalist, in 1938.

The Post-it Note was invented by 3M employee Spencer Silver in 1968.

The idea of the credit card was first implemented by Frank McNamara in 1950.

The first recorded patent for a safety razor was issued to King C. Gillette in 1904.

The concept of the jet engine was developed by Sir Frank Whittle in the 1930s.

The concept of GPS (Global Positioning System) was developed by the United States Department of Defense.

The first successful artificial heart transplant was performed by Dr. Robert Jarvik in 1982.

The concept of the barcode was invented by Norman Joseph Woodland in 1948.

The Slinky was invented by naval engineer Richard James in 1943.

Scotch tape was invented by Richard Drew in 1928.

The first synthetic plastic, Bakelite, was invented by Leo Baekeland in 1907.

The concept of the pacemaker was developed by John Hopps in 1950.

The first electric guitar was invented by Adolph Rickenbacker in 1931.

The concept of the computer hard disk drive was developed by IBM in 1956.

The first successful kidney transplant was performed by Dr. Joseph E. Murray in 1954.

The concept of the barcode was first implemented in a supermarket in Ohio in 1974.

The concept of the electric refrigerator was patented by Oliver Evans in 1805.

The concept of the electric toaster was patented by George Schneider in 1893.

The concept of the personal computer was popularized by IBM with the release of the IBM PC in 1981.

The first successful human heart transplant was performed by Dr. Christiaan Barnard in 1967.

The concept of the artificial heart was developed by Paul Winchell in 1963.

The first video game console, the Magnavox Odyssey, was released in 1972.

The concept of the digital camera was developed by Steven Sasson at Eastman Kodak in 1975.

The concept of the microwave oven was developed by Percy Spencer in 1945.

The first successful open-heart surgery was performed by Dr. Daniel Hale Williams in 1893.

The concept of the insulin pump was developed by Dean Kamen in 1976.

The concept of the internet was developed through the ARPANET project in the 1960s.

The concept of the artificial limb was developed by James Edward Hanger, the first documented amputee of the Civil War.

The concept of the pacemaker was patented by Wilson Greatbatch in 1960.

The concept of the air conditioner was developed by Willis Carrier in 1902.

The concept of the barometer was developed by Evangelista Torricelli in 1643.

The concept of the Geiger counter was developed by Hans Geiger in 1908.

The concept of the LASER (Light Amplification by Stimulated Emission of Radiation) was developed by Arthur Schawlow and Charles Townes in 1958.

The first successful organ transplant, a kidney, was performed by Dr. Joseph Murray in 1954.

The concept of the hearing aid was developed by Miller Reese Hutchison in 1898.

The concept of the typewriter was developed by Christopher Latham Sholes in 1868.

The concept of the sewing machine was developed by Elias Howe in 1846.

The concept of the electric fan was developed by Schuyler Skaats Wheeler in 1882.

The concept of the artificial kidney dialysis machine was developed by Willem Kolff in 1943.

The concept of the pacemaker was developed by Wilson Greatbatch in 1958.

The concept of the prosthetic limb was developed by Van Phillips in 1984.

The concept of the hearing aid was developed by Donald Schum in 1948.

The concept of the electric razor was developed by Jacob Schick in 1928.

The concept of the washing machine was developed by Alva J. Fisher in 1908.

The concept of the electric dishwasher was developed by Josephine Cochrane in 1886.

The concept of the first artificial heart was developed by Paul Winchell in 1952.

The concept of the defibrillator was developed by Dr. Claude Beck in 1947.

The concept of the respirator was developed by Forrest Bird in 1958.

The concept of the artificial limb was developed by Benjamin Franklin Palmer in 1846.

The concept of the respirator was developed by George Poe in 1928.

The concept of the dental drill was developed by George F. Green in 1875.

The concept of the electric blender was developed by Stephen J. Poplawski in 1922.

The concept of the artificial heart valve was developed by Albert Starr in 1960.

The concept of the heart-lung machine was developed by John H. Gibbon Jr. in 1935.

The concept of the artificial cornea was developed by Claes H. Dohlman in 1956.

The concept of the artificial pancreas was developed by Arnold Kadish in 1961.

The concept of the artificial blood was developed by Charles Drew in 1940.

The concept of the artificial liver was developed by William J. Kolff in 1956.

6

Movie

The first movie ever made is considered to be "Roundhay Garden Scene," filmed in 1888 by Louis Le Prince.

The longest film ever made is "Logistics" (2012), with a runtime of 51 days.

"Avatar" (2009) is the highest-grossing film of all time, surpassing $2.8 billion in worldwide box office revenue.

Alfred Hitchcock's "Psycho" (1960) was the first film to show a flushing toilet on screen.

The iconic shower scene in "Psycho" took seven days to shoot for just three minutes of screen time.

The word "smurf" is mentioned 534 times in "The Smurfs 2" (2013).

"Gone with the Wind" (1939) was the first color film to win the Best Picture Oscar.

The first feature-length animated film is "Snow White and the Seven Dwarfs" (1937).

The sound of the velociraptors in "Jurassic Park" (1993) is a combination of the sounds of tortoises mating and horses breathing.

The word "muggle" was added to the Oxford English Dictionary, thanks to J.K. Rowling's "Harry Potter" series.

"The Shawshank Redemption" (1994) initially performed poorly at the box office but became a classic after its home video release.

The first film to use the Wilhelm Scream was "Distant Drums" (1951), and it has since become a cinematic inside joke.

"The Matrix" (1999) popularized the use of "bullet time" slow-motion photography.

"The Dark Knight" (2008) was the first major Hollywood film to shoot in IMAX.

The "Star Wars" series was not originally planned as a trilogy; George Lucas had a larger saga in mind.

Marlon Brando memorized all his lines written on cue cards for "The Godfather" (1972) because he refused to read the script.

The "Lord of the Rings" trilogy used over 48,000 swords, axes, and other weapons during filming.

Stanley Kubrick's "The Shining" (1980) holds the record for the most retakes of a single scene, with 127 takes for the "Here's Johnny!" scene.

The "Rocky" film series was inspired by the real-life story of boxer Chuck Wepner.

Orson Welles' "Citizen Kane" (1941) is often considered one of the greatest films of all time.

"Forrest Gump" (1994) digitally inserted Tom Hanks into historical footage, creating the illusion of interaction with historical figures.

The first motion picture with synchronized sound is "The Jazz Singer" (1927).

The first use of computer-generated imagery (CGI) in a feature film was in "Westworld" (1973).

"E.T. the Extra-Terrestrial" (1982) featured an actual alien, not a puppet or CGI, designed by Carlo Rambaldi.

The "Harry Potter" film series employed over 25,000 individual special-effects shots.

The first film to win both the Best Picture and Best Animated Feature Oscars was "The Lord of the Rings: The Return of the King" (2003).

The "Mission: Impossible" film series is known for its intense stunts, with Tom Cruise performing many of his own, including scaling the Burj Khalifa in Dubai.

The word "robot" was introduced to the world in the play "R.U.R." (Rossum's Universal Robots) by Karel Čapek.

The original "King Kong" (1933) was the first film to have a synchronized musical score.

"Casablanca" (1942) was mostly filmed on a Hollywood set, with a small portion shot on location in Morocco.

The "Terminator" series popularized the phrase "I'll be back," spoken by Arnold Schwarzenegger.

The average length of a shot in a modern film is around 2.5 seconds, compared to 8 seconds in the 1930s.

"Titanic" (1997) had the largest budget of any film at the time, costing around $200 million to produce.

The film "Cleopatra" (1963) almost bankrupted 20th Century Fox due to its high production costs.

The first film to feature a kiss was "The Kiss" (1896), directed by William Heise.

"The Wizard of Oz" (1939) was one of the first films to use Technicolor, transitioning from black and white to color.

The iconic "Hasta la vista, baby" line from "Terminator 2: Judgment Day" (1991) became widely popular.

"The Exorcist" (1973) was the first horror film to be nominated for an Academy Award for Best Picture.

The "Toy Story" trilogy was the first to be entirely created using computer-generated imagery (CGI).

"Jaws" (1975) was the first film to gross over $100 million at the box office.

"The Terminator" (1984) was James Cameron's breakthrough film as a director.

The first feature-length animated film with synchronized sound is "Steamboat Willie" (1928), featuring Mickey Mouse.

The "Die Hard" series is known for its unconventional Christmas setting in the first film.

"Pulp Fiction" (1994) popularized nonlinear storytelling in mainstream cinema.

The "Indiana Jones" character was named after George Lucas's Alaskan Malamute dog.

The "Back to the Future" trilogy originally had a different time-traveling device, a refrigerator, instead of the iconic DeLorean car.

The film "Blade Runner" (1982) is based on Philip K. Dick's novel "Do Androids Dream of Electric Sheep?"

"The Silence of the Lambs" (1991) is the only horror film to win the Best Picture Oscar.

The "Fast and Furious" franchise is known for its elaborate and often unrealistic car stunts.

The "Twilight" series sparked a resurgence in vampire-themed films and TV shows.

"The Revenant" (2015) was primarily shot using natural light, creating a visually stunning cinematic experience.

The first film to use the word "vampire" was "Nosferatu" (1922).

"The Matrix" series popularized the concept of a simulated reality.

"The Princess Bride" (1987) was adapted from William Goldman's novel of the same name.

The iconic line "Here's looking at you, kid" from "Casablanca" (1942) was improvised by Humphrey Bogart.

The first use of 3D glasses in cinema dates back to the 1920s.

"The Sixth Sense" (1999) is known for its unexpected twist ending.

The "Die Hard" series was based on the novel "Nothing Lasts Forever" by Roderick Thorp.

The first feature film with synchronized dialogue was "The Jazz Singer" (1927).

"Inception" (2010) features a spinning top that becomes a symbol of reality within the film.

The first film to receive an X rating from the Motion Picture Association of America (MPAA) was "Midnight Cowboy" (1969).

The "Mad Max" series features practical effects and minimal CGI, emphasizing real stunts and explosions.

"The Matrix" series introduced the concept of "bullet time" slow-motion cinematography.

"Fight Club" (1999) is known for its unreliable narrator and unexpected plot twists.

The "Alien" series created iconic and influential designs, including the facehugger and chestburster.

"The Godfather" (1972) was based on the novel by Mario Puzo.

The "Ghostbusters" (1984) theme song became an iconic part of popular culture.

"The Lord of the Rings" trilogy was filmed simultaneously over 438 days.

The first feature film shot entirely on an iPhone was "Tangerine" (2015).

"The Social Network" (2010) depicted the founding of Facebook and is known for its rapid-fire dialogue and storytelling.

Message ChatGPT…

ChatGPT can make mistakes. Consider checking important

7

Planets

Mercury is the smallest planet in our solar system.

Venus rotates on its axis in the opposite direction to most planets.

Earth is the only known planet to support life.

Mars has the largest volcano in the solar system, Olympus Mons.

Jupiter is the largest planet and has a storm called the Great Red Spot.

Saturn's rings are made mostly of ice particles and dust.

Uranus is tilted on its side, and its rings are perpendicular to its orbit.

Neptune has the strongest winds in the solar system.

Pluto was reclassified as a "dwarf planet" in 2006.

There are more than 200 moons in our solar system.

Ganymede, a moon of Jupiter, is the largest moon in the solar system.

Titan, a moon of Saturn, has a thick atmosphere and lakes of liquid methane.

The Kuiper Belt is a region of the solar system beyond Neptune, containing many small, icy bodies.

The Oort Cloud is a hypothetical region of icy bodies even farther from the sun than the Kuiper Belt.

The sun makes up about 99.86% of the mass of the solar system.

A day on Venus is longer than a year on Venus.

Earth is the only planet not named after a god.

Mars has the tallest volcano and the deepest canyon in the solar system.

Jupiter has at least 79 known moons.

Saturn's density is low enough that it could float in water (if there was a big enough bathtub).

Uranus and Neptune are classified as "ice giants" due to their composition.

Neptune was the first planet discovered through mathematical predictions.

Mercury has extreme temperature variations, with scorching days and freezing nights.

The moon is gradually moving away from Earth.

Mars has the largest dust storms in the solar system.

Venus has a retrograde rotation, meaning it rotates backward compared to most planets.

Io, a moon of Jupiter, is the most volcanically active object in the solar system.

The largest volcano on Mars, Olympus Mons, is about three times the height of Mount Everest.

The Great Red Spot on Jupiter has been observed since the 17th century.

Saturn's rings are divided into seven major groups.

Uranus has a faint ring system discovered in 1977.

Neptune's atmosphere has the fastest winds in the solar system, reaching speeds of 1,500 miles per hour.

Pluto was discovered in 1930 by astronomer Clyde Tombaugh.

Jupiter's magnetic field is 14 times stronger than Earth's.

Saturn's moon Enceladus has geysers of water vapor erupting from its surface.

The largest moon of Neptune, Triton, orbits in the opposite direction of the planet's rotation.

The asteroid belt is located between the orbits of Mars and Jupiter.

Earth's atmosphere is about 78% nitrogen and 21% oxygen.

Mars has the largest volcano in the solar system, Olympus Mons.

The rings of Saturn are made up of billions of particles, ranging in size from tiny dust grains to large chunks.

The largest known volcano in the solar system is on Mars, named Olympus Mons.

A year on Neptune is equivalent to about 165 Earth years.

Io, a moon of Jupiter, experiences tidal heating due to gravitational interactions with Jupiter and other moons.

The surface of Venus is hot enough to melt lead.

The sun's gravity holds the entire solar system together.

The Hubble Space Telescope has provided detailed images of distant planets and galaxies.

The largest volcano on Earth is Mauna Loa in Hawaii.

The sun contains about 99.8% of the total mass of the entire solar system.

The atmosphere of Venus is mainly composed of carbon dioxide, with clouds of sulfuric acid.

The dwarf planet Eris is slightly smaller than Pluto but more massive.

Mars has the largest canyon in the solar system, Valles Marineris.

Titan, a moon of Saturn, has a thick atmosphere that obscures its surface from direct view.

Neptune was discovered in 1846, based on mathematical predictions by Urbain Le Verrier and Johann Galle.

The Milky Way galaxy, our home, contains billions of stars.

The first successful mission to Mars was NASA's Viking 1, which landed in 1976.

The moon's gravitational pull causes tides on Earth.

Earth's magnetic field is generated by the movement of molten iron and nickel in its core.

Venus rotates so slowly on its axis that a day on Venus is longer than a year.

The surface temperature of Mercury varies dramatically, from extremely hot to extremely cold.

Jupiter has a faint ring system composed of four main rings.

The atmospheres of Uranus and Neptune contain methane, giving them a blue tint.

The spacecraft Voyager 1 is the farthest human-made object from Earth, traveling into interstellar space.

The largest moon of Saturn, Titan, has a thick atmosphere and lakes of liquid methane and ethane.

Pluto has five known moons, including Charon, its largest moon.

The sun will eventually exhaust its nuclear fuel and expand into a red giant before becoming a white dwarf.

The asteroid Ceres, located in the asteroid belt, is classified as both an asteroid and a dwarf planet.

The sun's equator rotates faster than its poles.

Venus has a day longer than its year, taking about 243 Earth days to complete one rotation.

Earth is the only known planet where water exists in all three states: solid, liquid, and gas.

The New Horizons spacecraft provided the first close-up images of Pluto in 2015, revealing diverse surface features.

8

Country

Canada has the longest coastline in the world, stretching over 202,080 kilometers.

The Great Wall of China is not visible from space with the naked eye, contrary to popular belief.

Norway is home to the Midnight Sun, where the sun doesn't set for several weeks during summer.

Australia is both a country and a continent, making it the world's smallest continent and the sixth-largest country.

Japan consists of over 6,800 islands.

The Maldives is the lowest country in the world, with an average ground level of just 1.5 meters above sea level.

Russia spans 11 time zones, making it the country with the most time zones.

Iceland has no mosquitoes.

Brazil is home to the Amazon Rainforest, often referred to as the "lungs of the Earth."

The world's largest desert is Antarctica.

Egypt is home to the pyramids, with the Great Pyramid of Giza being one of the Seven Wonders of the Ancient World.

The Vatican City is the smallest independent state in the world.

Mongolia is the least densely populated country on Earth.

Finland has the highest concentration of lakes in the world.

New Zealand is home to the only alpine parrot, the Kea.

The United States is the third-largest country by land area.

Kenya is home to the Great Rift Valley, a massive geological formation.

Greenland is the world's largest island but has the lowest population density.

Singapore is the only island city-state in the world.

France is the most visited country globally.

India has the world's second-largest population.

South Korea has the fastest internet speed in the world.

Argentina is home to the widest avenue, Avenida 9 de Julio, in Buenos Aires.

Spain has the second-highest number of UNESCO World Heritage Sites.

The Netherlands is one of the world's largest exporters of flowers, particularly tulips.

Switzerland is famous for its numerous lakes, with Lake Geneva being one of the largest.

Thailand is known for its floating markets, where vendors sell goods from boats.

Mount Everest, the world's highest peak, is located on the border of Nepal and China.

The Philippines has the most active volcanoes in Asia.

Germany is known for its Autobahn, a highway system without a general speed limit.

Mexico City is one of the most populous cities in the world.

Madagascar is home to unique wildlife, including lemurs.

South Africa is known for the Table Mountain in Cape Town.

Peru is home to Machu Picchu, an ancient Incan city.

Sweden has a "Freedom to Roam" concept, allowing people to access most public and private land freely.

Turkey is located on two continents: Europe and Asia.

Saudi Arabia is the birthplace of Islam and home to Mecca.

Vietnam is famous for its limestone karst landscapes.

The United Kingdom is made up of four countries: England, Scotland, Wales, and Northern Ireland.

Israel has the lowest point on Earth, the Dead Sea.

China is the world's most populous country.

Nigeria is the most populous country in Africa.

Cuba is known for its classic cars, remnants of the pre-revolution era.

Chile has the longest north-south stretch of land of any country.

The Bahamas has one of the world's deepest ocean sinkholes, Dean's Blue Hole.

Bangladesh is the most densely populated large country in the world.

The Great Barrier Reef in Australia is the largest coral reef system.

Austria is famous for its classical music composers, including Mozart and Beethoven.

Iran has one of the world's oldest continuous major civilizations.

Canada has more lakes than the rest of the world combined.

The Taj Mahal in India is considered one of the most beautiful buildings in the world.

Peru is home to the source of the Amazon River.

Japan experiences around 1,500 earthquakes annually.

Kenya is known for its diverse wildlife, including the "Big Five" – lion, elephant, buffalo, leopard, and rhinoceros.

Greece has a coastline of approximately 13,600 kilometers due to its numerous islands.

The United States has the world's longest road network.

Malaysia is one of the world's largest producers of palm oil.

Sweden has the highest percentage of households with internet access in the European Union.

Greenland is part of the Kingdom of Denmark but has a high degree of self-governance.

Ecuador is named after the equator, which runs through the country.

Morocco is home to the ancient city of Marrakech, known for its vibrant markets.

Mongolia is known for its vast steppes and nomadic culture.

Egypt has the oldest known dress in the world, dating back over 5,000 years.

Brazil has the largest Japanese population outside of Japan.

Australia is home to the world's longest fence, the Dingo Fence.

China is the world's largest producer of rice.

Iceland has no army, navy, or air force.

Italy has the most UNESCO World Heritage Sites.

Ghana was the first African country to gain independence from colonial rule.

Thailand is known for its unique floating lantern festivals.

9

History

Cleopatra, the last Pharaoh of Egypt, lived closer in time to the moon landing than to the construction of the Great Pyramid.

The Great Wall of China is not visible from the moon with the naked eye, contrary to popular belief.

The ancient city of Rome had public toilets with a common sponge on a stick for everyone to use.

The city of Istanbul was formerly known as Byzantium and later as Constantinople before being renamed.

The world's oldest known map is from Catalhoyuk, dating back to around 6200 BC.

The Library of Alexandria in ancient Egypt housed countless scrolls and was considered the largest library of the ancient world.

The concept of zero in mathematics was developed by Indian mathematicians around the 5th century.

The Black Death, which swept through Europe in the 14th century, wiped out an estimated 75-200 million people.

The first recorded Olympic Games were held in ancient Greece in 776 BC.

Ancient Egyptians used honey as a form of currency.

The Eiffel Tower was originally intended to be a temporary installation for the 1889 World's Fair in Paris.

The ancient city of Troy, from Homer's Iliad, is now believed to have existed and been excavated in modern-day Turkey.

Leonardo da Vinci could write with one hand while simultaneously drawing with the other.

The Great Fire of London in 1666 was sparked in a bakery on Pudding Lane.

The concept of time zones was first proposed by Sir Sandford Fleming at the International Meridian Conference in 1884.

The Great Emu War occurred in Australia in 1932, where soldiers were sent to combat a large population of emus with machine guns.

The Taj Mahal was built by the Mughal Emperor Shah Jahan in memory of his wife Mumtaz Mahal.

The Mayan civilization used a symbol for zero in their mathematics long before it was adopted in other cultures.

The shortest war in history was between Britain and Zanzibar in 1896, lasting only 38 minutes.

The first recorded use of the term "O.K." was in 1839, in the Boston Morning Post.

The city of Venice, Italy, is built on a network of canals and is known for its absence of cars.

The Incas used a system of knotted strings called quipus for record-keeping.

The concept of democracy originated in ancient Greece in the city-state of Athens.

The world's oldest known board game, Senet, was played in ancient Egypt around 3100 BC.

The Great Pyramid of Giza was originally covered in smooth, white Tura limestone, making it shine in the sun.

The first known reference to a vending machine is from the first-century work of Hero of Alexandria.

The ancient city of Petra in Jordan was carved directly into rose-red cliffs.

The invention of the wheel is believed to have occurred around 3500 BC in Mesopotamia.

The Gutenberg Bible, printed in the 15th century, was the first major book printed using mass-produced movable metal type in Europe.

The ancient city of Babylon had one of the earliest codes of law, the Code of Hammurabi.

The largest empire in history was the Mongol Empire, which spanned over 9 million square miles.

The Great Sphinx of Giza is believed to have been built during the reign of Pharaoh Khafre.

The Battle of Marathon in 490 BC inspired the modern marathon race.

The Rosetta Stone played a crucial role in deciphering ancient Egyptian hieroglyphs.

The Vikings used a sun compass, called a "sundial," for navigation.

The term "Hijack" originated in the 1920s when cars were being stolen during prohibition in the United States.

The Hanging Gardens of Babylon, one of the Seven Wonders of the Ancient World, may have never existed.

The first known recorded war, the Battle of Megiddo, occurred in 1479 BC.

The Russian mystic Rasputin survived being poisoned, shot multiple times, and finally drowned in 1916.

The Great Wall of China was not built in a single continuous line but in several sections by different dynasties.

The famous gunfight at the O.K. Corral in 1881 lasted only about 30 seconds.

The concept of a weekend, with Saturday and Sunday off, was introduced by the labor movement in the early 20th century.

The concept of paper money was first developed in China during the Tang Dynasty (618-907 AD).

The ancient city of Machu Picchu was not known to the Western world until its discovery by Hiram Bingham in 1911.

The Battle of Gettysburg during the American Civil War had the highest number of casualties over a three-day period.

The oldest known map of the stars is a prehistoric cave painting found in France.

The Great Famine of 1315-1317 was one of the worst periods of food shortage in medieval Europe.

The shortest reigning pope in history was Pope Urban VII, who served for only 13 days in 1590.

The term "bikini" for a two-piece swimsuit was named after the Bikini Atoll, the site of atomic bomb testing.

The Industrial Revolution began in England in the late 18th century, leading to significant social and economic changes.

The Mona Lisa was stolen from the Louvre in 1911 but was recovered two years later.

The first recorded mention of the city of Rome is in the Iliad by Homer.

The Berlin Wall, which separated East and West Berlin, fell in 1989, marking the end of the Cold War.

The Wright brothers' first successful powered flight in 1903 lasted only 12 seconds.

The concept of a round Earth was proposed by ancient Greek philosophers, including Pythagoras and Aristotle.

The world's first computer programmer was Ada Lovelace, who worked with Charles Babbage's analytical engine in the 19th century.

The first known organized team sport was ancient Egyptian field hockey around 2000 BC.

The longest-ruling monarch in European history was King Louis XIV of France, who reigned for 72 years.

The concept of human rights can be traced back to the Cyrus Cylinder, a clay cylinder from ancient Persia.

The Pacific island of Nauru was once the wealthiest nation per capita due to its phosphate reserves.

The ancient Greeks used a device called an "Antikythera mechanism" for astronomical calculations.

The word "assassin" has its roots in the medieval Nizari Ismailis, a group known for political killings.

The Great Fire of Rome in AD 64 was famously blamed on Emperor Nero, who allegedly played the lyre while the city burned.

The first known use of the term "computer bug" occurred in 1947 when a moth caused a malfunction in an early computer.

The Silk Road, a network of trade routes, connected the East and West for centuries.

The Battle of Thermopylae in 480 BC, made famous by the movie "300," was a key conflict during the Greco-Persian Wars.

The first known coins were minted in Lydia (modern-day Turkey) around 600 BC.

The Great Fire of 1666 in London led to the rebuilding of the city with wider streets and brick houses.

The ancient city of Carthage was a powerful rival to Rome and engaged in the Punic Wars.

The concept of the metric system was proposed during the French Revolution and later adopted globally.

10

Science

The speed of light is approximately 299,792 kilometers per second.

Honey never spoils. Archaeologists have found pots of honey in ancient Egyptian tombs that are over 3,000 years old and still perfectly edible.

A day on Venus is longer than a year on Venus. It takes about 243 Earth days for Venus to complete one rotation on its axis, but only about 225 Earth days to orbit the Sun.

There are more possible iterations of a game of chess than there are atoms in the observable universe.

Octopuses have three hearts. Two pump blood to the gills, and one pumps it to the rest of the body.

The Earth's core is hotter than the surface of the sun.

The human brain is more active during sleep than during the day when awake.

A teaspoon of neutron star material would weigh about six billion tons.

Jupiter's massive gravity has a protective effect on Earth, helping to deflect potential asteroid impacts.

The majority of the gold on Earth comes from massive stellar explosions, called supernovae.

The universe is estimated to be around 13.8 billion years old.

The majority of the world's oxygen is produced by the ocean, not by forests.

One tablespoon of a neutron star would weigh about 6 billion tons.

There are more bacteria in your mouth than there are people on Earth.

Atoms are 99.9999999% empty space.

A single rainforest can produce 20% of the Earth's oxygen.

The world's largest desert is Antarctica.

The smell of freshly-cut grass is a plant distress call.

The human nose can remember 50,000 different scents.

Dolphins have names for each other.

Cows have best friends and can become stressed when they are separated.

If you unravelled all the DNA in your body, it would stretch from the Earth to the Sun and back over 600 times.

The sun makes up 99.86% of the solar system's mass.

The largest volcano in the solar system is on Mars and is called Olympus Mons.

There are more stars in the universe than grains of sand on all the beaches on Earth.

The Great Wall of China is not visible from the moon with the naked eye.

A day on Pluto is less than 7 hours long.

An asteroid impact is responsible for the extinction of the dinosaurs.

The Eiffel Tower can be 15 cm taller during the summer due to thermal expansion.

The human body has more bacteria cells than human cells.

Lightning can strike the same place twice.

The average person walks the equivalent of three times around the world in a lifetime.

The first known form of life on Earth was bacteria that lived 3.5 billion years ago.

A day on Mars is only about 24.6 hours.

There are more possible iterations of a game of chess than there are atoms in the observable universe.

The fingerprints of koala bears are virtually indistinguishable from those of humans, so much so that they could be confused at a crime scene.

The only planet in our solar system that rotates clockwise is Venus.

The largest volcano in our solar system is on Mars, called Olympus Mons.

The world's largest ocean is the Pacific Ocean, covering more than 63 million square miles.

Honey never spoils. Archaeologists have found pots of honey in ancient Egyptian tombs that are over 3,000 years old and still perfectly edible.

A day on Venus is longer than a year on Venus. It takes about 243 Earth days for Venus to complete one rotation on its axis, but only about 225 Earth days to orbit the Sun.

Sound cannot travel through a vacuum, which is why there is no sound in space.

The coldest natural temperature ever directly recorded at ground level on Earth is −128.6 °F (−89.2 °C) at the Soviet Union's Vostok Station in Antarctica.

A neutron star is so dense that a sugar-cube-sized amount of its material would weigh about one billion tons on Earth.

The Earth is not a perfect sphere; it is slightly flattened at the poles and bulging at the equator due to its rotation.

Bananas are berries, but strawberries aren't.

A single rainforest can produce 20% of the Earth's oxygen.

There is a planet named 55 Cancri e, which is twice the size of Earth and eight times its mass, and it's made of diamond.

The word "nerd" was first coined by Dr. Seuss in "If I Ran the Zoo" in 1950.

A nanosecond, one billionth of a second, is about the time it takes for light to travel 30 centimeters in a vacuum.

The smell of rain is called "petrichor."

A day on Mercury (one full rotation on its axis) is longer than its year (orbit around the Sun).

The world's oldest known creature, the "Ming the clam," lived to be over 500 years old.

The electric chair was invented by a dentist.

Cows have best friends and can become stressed when they are separated.

The average cloud weighs about 1.1 million pounds.

The total weight of all the ants on Earth is comparable to that of all the humans on Earth.

The International Space Station travels at a speed of about 28,000 kilometers per hour (17,500 miles per hour).

The shortest war in history was between Britain and Zanzibar on August 27, 1896, lasting only 38 minutes.

There is a species of jellyfish, Turritopsis dohrnii, that is biologically immortal. It can revert its cells back to their earliest form and start its life cycle anew.

The word "astronaut" means "star sailor" in its origin.

The largest desert in the world is Antarctica.

The human brain generates about 20 watts of electrical power while awake, enough to power a dim light bulb.

The Milky Way galaxy is on a collision course with the Andromeda galaxy, but this collision won't happen for about 4 billion years.

The shortest war in history was between Britain and Zanzibar on August 27, 1896, lasting only 38 minutes.

The longest time a person has ever survived without sleep is 11 days.

The probability of being killed by a falling coconut is about 1 in 250 million.

The speed of Earth's rotation is gradually slowing down due to tidal forces.

A group of flamingos is called a "flamboyance."

If you could fold a piece of paper in half 42 times, it would reach the moon.

11

Strange creatures

The Axolotl, also known as the Mexican walking fish, can regrow entire limbs and even parts of its heart and brain.

The immortal jellyfish can revert its cells to their earliest form and start its life cycle anew.

The mimic octopus can imitate the appearance and behavior of various marine animals, including lionfish, flatfish, and sea snakes.

The yeti crab, discovered near hydrothermal vents, cultivates bacteria on its hairy claws and uses them for nutrition.

The tardigrade, or water bear, can survive extreme conditions such as radiation, vacuum of space, and boiling temperatures.

The Kakapo, a nocturnal parrot from New Zealand, is the heaviest parrot and unable to fly.

The mantis shrimp has one of the most complex eyes in the animal kingdom, capable of seeing polarized light and a wide spectrum of colors.

The axolotl and the olm are neotenic salamanders that retain their aquatic juvenile characteristics throughout their lives.

The immortal jellyfish can potentially live forever by reverting its cells to their earliest stage when faced with aging or injury.

The platypus is one of the few mammals that lay eggs and produce milk but lacks nipples.

The Portuguese Man o' War, often mistaken for a jellyfish, is a colony of organisms working together.

The fangtooth fish has the largest teeth in proportion to its body size of any fish in the ocean.

The blobfish looks drastically different in its natural deep-sea habitat compared to its appearance when brought to the surface.

The mimicry of the leaf-tailed gecko allows it to blend seamlessly with tree bark, making it almost invisible to predators.

The axolotl is known for its exceptional regenerative abilities, capable of regrowing not only limbs but also parts of its heart and brain.

The okapi, native to the Democratic Republic of Congo, is the only living relative of the giraffe.

The pink fairy armadillo is the smallest species of armadillo, known for its vibrant pink armor.

The Aye-Aye, a lemur native to Madagascar, uses its long, thin middle finger to extract insects from tree bark.

The hammerhead shark's unique head shape allows it to have a wider range of vision than other sharks.

The flying snake can glide through the air by flattening its body into a concave shape.

The narwhal's long tusk is actually an elongated tooth that can reach lengths of up to 10 feet.

The lyrebird can mimic natural and artificial sounds, including chainsaws and camera shutters.

The peacock mantis shrimp has the fastest strike in the animal kingdom, capable of reaching speeds of 23 meters per second.

The axolotl is often referred to as the "Mexican walking fish," even though it is a salamander and not a fish.

The mimic octopus is a master of disguise, imitating the appearance and behaviors of various marine animals to avoid predators.

The fangtooth fish, despite its fearsome appearance, is a small deep-sea fish that rarely grows longer than 6 inches.

The mantis shrimp's eyes have 16 types of color receptors, compared to only three in humans, allowing them to see a broader spectrum of colors.

The okapi's striped hindquarters and front legs help it blend into the dense vegetation of its rainforest habitat.

The axolotl and the olm are both neotenic salamanders, meaning they retain their aquatic juvenile features throughout their lives.

The immortal jellyfish can revert its cells to their earliest stage, essentially aging backward and potentially achieving biological immortality.

The platypus is known for its electrolocation ability, which allows it to detect the electric fields generated by the muscles and nerves of its prey.

The Portuguese Man o' War is a colonial organism made up of specialized polyps working together, each with a specific function.

The lyrebird's impressive vocal mimicry includes imitating the sounds of other birds, chainsaws, camera shutters, and even car alarms.

The axolotl's regenerative abilities extend to various body parts, making it a subject of scientific interest in regenerative medicine.

The mimic octopus has been observed imitating the appearance and movements of lionfish, flatfish, and sea snakes to deter predators.

The fangtooth fish's large, sharp teeth are adapted for catching and holding onto small, elusive prey in the deep-sea environment.

The blobfish's gelatinous appearance is due to its lack of a swim bladder, which helps fish maintain buoyancy in water.

The axolotl's ability to regrow complex structures like limbs and organs has sparked interest in potential applications for human regenerative medicine.

The okapi's long tongue, which can reach lengths of up to 18 inches, helps it strip leaves from trees to feed.

The Aye-Aye's elongated middle finger is used to tap on tree bark and detect hollow spaces where insects may be hiding.

The narwhal's tusk is actually an elongated tooth that grows in a spiral pattern and can reach lengths of up to 10 feet.

The flying snake's ability to glide through the air is facilitated by its flattened body and lateral undulation.

The lyrebird's elaborate tail feathers are used in courtship displays to attract mates.

The peacock mantis shrimp's powerful strike is so fast that it creates cavitation bubbles, leading to a burst of light and heat.

The axolotl's unique appearance includes feathery external gills and a wide, smiling mouth.

The mimic octopus's ability to mimic the appearance and behaviors of other marine animals serves as a form of defense against predators.

The fangtooth fish is adapted to the extreme conditions of the deep sea, where food is scarce and pressure is high.

The mantis shrimp's eyes can move independently of each other, providing a wide field of vision.

The okapi's distinctive appearance, with zebra-like stripes on its hindquarters, helps it blend into its forest surroundings.

The immortal jellyfish's ability to reverse its aging process has implications for research into aging and cellular regeneration.

The platypus is one of the few venomous mammals, with males possessing venomous spurs on their hind limbs.

The Portuguese Man o' War's tentacles can deliver a painful sting to humans, and its venomous cells can cause welts and respiratory distress.

The lyrebird's incredible vocal mimicry has led to its reputation as one of the best imitators in the animal kingdom.

The axolotl's regeneration abilities have inspired research into understanding and harnessing regenerative processes in other animals.

The mimic octopus's repertoire of imitations includes appearing like flatfish, lionfish, and sea snakes to avoid predation.

The fangtooth fish's large teeth are adapted for catching and holding onto elusive prey in the deep-sea environment.

The blobfish's appearance changes drastically when brought to the surface due to the difference in pressure.

The Aye-Aye's unique hunting method involves tapping on tree bark and using its specialized middle finger to extract insects.

The narwhal's tusk is believed to play a role in communication and sensory perception in the Arctic environment.

The flying snake's ability to glide through the air allows it to travel between trees in search of prey.

The lyrebird's elaborate tail feathers play a crucial role in its courtship displays to attract potential mates.

The peacock mantis shrimp's powerful strike is one of the fastest movements in the animal kingdom.

The axolotl's external gills help it breathe underwater, and its ability to regenerate them is vital for long-term survival.

The mimic octopus's mimicry is not solely for defensive purposes; it also uses it for hunting and approaching prey.

The fangtooth fish's large teeth are so prominent that it has difficulty closing its mouth fully.

The mantis shrimp's eyes can detect polarized light, and its color vision is far more advanced than that of humans.

The okapi's tongue is prehensile, allowing it to grasp and strip leaves from trees more efficiently.

The immortal jellyfish's ability to revert its cells has led scientists to study it for potential insights into human aging and regenerative medicine.

The platypus's electrolocation ability helps it detect prey in murky water, giving it an advantage in hunting.

The Portuguese Man o' War's sting can be painful to humans, and in rare cases, it can lead to more severe reactions such as respiratory distress.